MAJOR TAYLOR
WORLD CYCLING CHAMPION

CHARLES R. SMITH JR.   ILLUSTRATED BY LEO ESPINOSA

CANDLEWICK PRESS

DECEMBER 7, 1896

"Welcome, cycling fans,
to the Garden Six-Day Race
here at Madison Square Garden!

"Who will rise to the challenge to ride the most laps over six days?
Who can withstand this test of physical endurance?
This test of mental strength?
This ultimate test of will and heart?
In six days, we shall see.
Good luck, gentlemen."

"Are the timers ready?
Are the starters ready?"

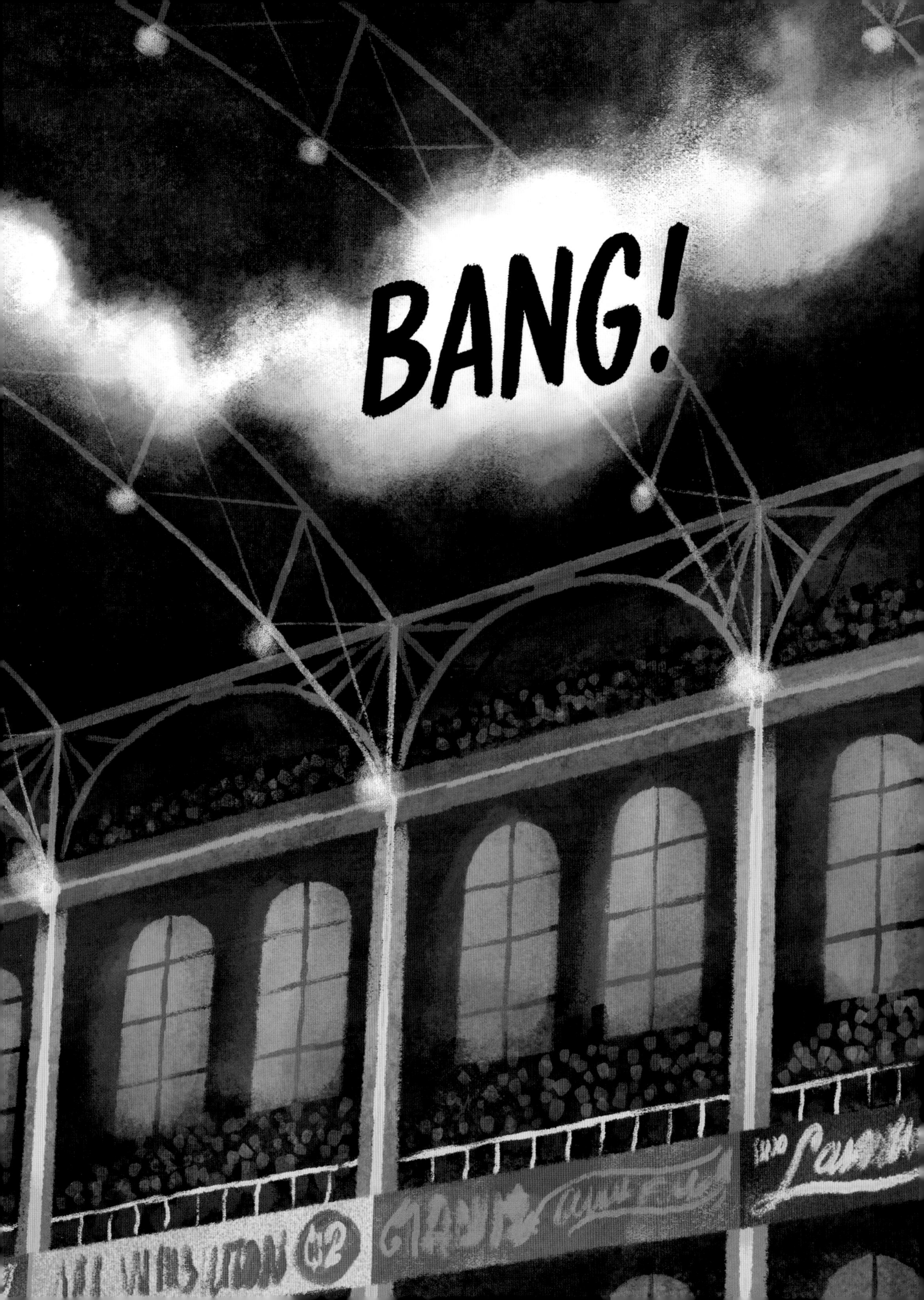
BANG!

GO, MAJOR, GO,
spin, Major, spin,
pump those legs, Major,
to propel you like the wind.

Faster and faster
and faster around the track,
pump those legs, Major,
to break away from the pack.

Just an eighteen-year-old boy
racing against men,
pedal, Major, pedal,
make those wheels spin.

Spin through the straight

spin up the turn

spin down the bend

spin spin with speed to burn.

One lap
two laps
ten laps
a mile
and another
and another
and another hundred more,

300 miles, Major, by hour 24!

DAY 2

Lap after lap
putting on a display
of blazing speed
you first showed one day
just a few months ago
right after a pro race,
when you snuck on a track
with timers still in place
and took off on your bike
at a whirlwind pace.

When you chased a new
record in the mile,
you attempted and broke
the record in style,
going eight seconds faster
than the white rider who
just set the record,
but then the officials banned you,
because you weren't allowed
on the Indianapolis track—
it was for white riders only
and you, Major, were Black.

So keep riding, Major,
just keep riding, Major.

Now that you're here
show you belong, Major.

The first Black face
in a pro bike race,
GO, MAJOR, GO,
stay with the pace!
Around and around
and around the track,
pump those legs, Major,
to stay away from the pack.
Pump-pump those legs, Major,
as they try to bump you,
pump-pump-pump harder
as they try to trap you.
Go faster go faster
so they can't catch you—
GO, MAJOR, GO,
don't let them crash you!

Just keep spinning, Major,
sliding through the wind
on the straight
up the curve
and down the bend again.

DAY 3

Keep spinning, Major,
like your first long-distance race,
just last year
when you started in last place.

75 miles
beginning to end,
just sixteen years old
no one thought you could win.

When the other racers saw
the color of your face,
they taunted you
and threatened you
to drive you from the race.
But you pedaled on, Major,
and you didn't quit,
and when the rain came
only you finished it.

So keep riding, Major,
keep riding, don't quit.
Now, just like then,
keep pedaling, finish it.

Compete like your very first
race five years ago,
when your boss at the bike shop
wanted you to show
what his bikes could do
in a ten-mile race,
but you said no
with a look of fear on your face.
But he said, "Just do your best.
Pedal until you get tired."

And when you saw the gold medal prize
you became inspired
and not only finished
all 10 miles, you won!
Your very first race,
by six seconds, you won!

So keep spinning, Major,
keep spinning, don't stop.
Stay focused, Major,
stay awake, don't drop.

DAY 4

One hour of sleep
for every eight on the bike
kept you in the race,
but you fought to stay upright.

Across your handlebars
a pillow was placed for your chest
to lean on so you could pedal
while still getting some rest.
Dodging and weaving
your way through the pack
as other riders collided
and crashed on the track,
your eyes started seeing things
as you fought to stay awake,
and soon it was hard to tell
what was real and what was fake.

DAY 5

By the fifth day only you
and thirteen riders remained,
each fighting to stay awake
with every muscle drained.
Belly empty
eyes heavy
joints aching
muscles sore—
all led to a

CRASH!

skidding you twenty feet across the floor.

The crowd gasped
as your limp body lay,
wondering would you, Major Taylor,
make it to the sixth day.

The same crowd that laughed
when you rolled onto the track,
the same crowd that taunted you
because you were Black,
was now chanting your name
with energy and zeal
to get up and go
to get back on your wheel.

**"MA-JOR!
MA-JOR!
MA-JOR!"**

But before you became Major
first you were Marshall,
just a boy performing
for crowds on your bicycle,
and those crowds gathered
at your job at the bike store
watching you do tricks
in a uniform you wore.
A military jacket that
made you stand out
made you look regal
gave you some clout,
so they called you "Major"
because you commanded attention
when you performed on your bike
with speed and precision.

Now here in New York,
the crowd chants your name
because of how far you came,
so get up, Major Taylor—
get back on your frame.

DAY 6

With the end in sight
you got your wheels spinning
entering the last day
with 1,524 miles ridden.

But each lap around the track
became harder and harder,
so you reached down deep
to go farther and farther.
You reached down deep
thinking of those who taunted you
but also those who supported you
like your family
your friends
and your coach, Birdie, too.
A former champion himself,
he saw a champion in you.

When others only saw color
Birdie saw what you could do,
so push, Major, push
for all of those who
cheered along the way
and believed in you.

Get those wheels spinning
around the track fast
up the curve
around the bend—

WATCH OUT, MAJOR!

A two-bike crash
left you lying in a heap,

body bruised

knees swollen

falling fast asleep,

unable to wake,

which meant your race was done,
just thirty minutes from finishing
but you, Major, were done.

Done in the race
but your career had just begun.
Going over 1,700 miles,
Major, you had a good run
finishing eighth out of twenty-eight
but you would soon become

MAJOR TAYLOR: WORLD CYCLING CHAMPION!

MAJOR'S STORY

Marshall Walter Taylor was born on November 26, 1878, in Indianapolis, Indiana. With eight children to feed, Marshall's father, Gilbert, took a job as a coachman, taking care of the horses and driving the carriage for the Southard family.

The Southards were a wealthy white family with one child, named Dan. He was eight years old, just like Marshall at the time, and the two became fast friends. Since they got along so well, the Southard family hired Marshall as a companion for Dan. Marshall lived with the family for weeks at a time. Dan had private tutors, and Marshall sat alongside him in his lessons. Marshall gained an education, along with confidence in his physical abilities from playing sports with Dan and his friends. Marshall learned at a young age that he could compete against anyone, regardless of color.

Life as Marshall knew it changed when the Southard family moved to Chicago. Dan gifted Marshall his own bike as a going-away present. That bike gave Marshall, now thirteen, the freedom to go where he wanted, when he wanted. Marshall used the bike to deliver newspapers to bring in money for his family. When he wasn't working, he was teaching himself tricks on his bike.

One day, Marshall's tricks caught the eye of a local bike shop owner. The owner hired him to sweep and clean up but mostly to attract customers by performing on his bike. Marshall was given the nickname "Major" because of the military jacket he wore while riding his bike.

Word of Marshall's talents traveled to former cycling champion Louis "Birdie" Munger. He was starting his own bicycle company and hired Marshall as his personal assistant. Birdie was so impressed with Marshall's curiosity and dedication to cycling that he began training him. When people asked who he was, Birdie replied, "The future champion."

Marshall took to his training, showing record-breaking speed in the sprint races. Unfortunately, Indiana didn't allow Black and white racers to compete together. So Birdie and Marshall moved to Worcester, Massachusetts, where all racers were invited to compete, regardless of color.

Birdie wanted Marshall to make a splash as a pro, so they began training for the Six-Day Race at Madison Square Garden in New York City. The popular endurance race would take place just after Marshall's eighteenth birthday.

When he rolled onto the track, Marshall was the lone Black racer in a field of twenty-eight. He was also the youngest and smallest. No one knew who he was when the race started. But when it was over, the cycling world knew the name Major Taylor.

As a pro, Major won races and set countless records along the way. Many of the white racers tried to hurt him on the track due to his skin color, but Marshall adapted racing tactics to avoid harm and emerge victorious. He would stay at the back until the last lap, then put on a quick burst of speed to sprint ahead for the victory. This racing style made him a fan favorite.

Major won the one-mile sprint at the track cycling world championship in 1899 in Montreal, Canada, making him the first African American to win a world championship in cycling and only the second Black athlete to become a champion in any sport.

In 1902, Major married Daisy Morris. Two years later, on May 11, Daisy gave birth to their only child. The baby girl was born in Sydney, Australia, where Major was competing, so they named her Sydney.

Unfortunately, when the automobile came into existence, the cycling world began to fade. And so did Major. In 1928, he put his money into an autobiography, *The Fastest Bicycle Rider in the World*. Two years later, he moved alone to a YMCA in Chicago to sell his book. He wasn't able to make enough money from his book sales, and the stock market crash of 1932 and bad deals wiped out most of his winnings. By the time he died on June 21, 1932, at the age of fifty-three, he was penniless. Major was buried in an unmarked grave outside of Chicago.

But his story does not end there. In 1948, when it became known that the great cycling champion Marshall "Major" Taylor was buried in an unmarked grave, a group of former pro bike racers used money donated by Frank Schwinn, owner of the Schwinn bicycle company, to exhume Major's body and move him to a proper burial site in Mount Greenwood Cemetery in Illinois. To celebrate his life and accomplishments, his gravesite marker reads: "World's champion bicycle rider who came up the hard way without hatred in his heart, an honest, courageous, and God-fearing, clean-living gentlemanly athlete. A credit to his race who always gave out his best. Gone but not forgotten."

Indeed. Gone but not forgotten, Major.

MAJOR'S MILESTONES

1892: Aged thirteen, Marshall reluctantly enters his first race, a ten-mile road race, with urging from his boss at the bike store. He wins!

June 30, 1895: Aged sixteen, Marshall enters his first long-distance race. The seventy-five-mile race goes from Indianapolis to Matthews, Indiana. Over fifty racers entered. Rain and muddy conditions stopped other racers, while only Marshall finished.

August 18, 1896: Aged seventeen, Marshall sneaks onto the brand-new Capital City Track after a pro race and officially (yet unofficially) breaks Walter Sanger's one-mile sprint record. Though several timers all recorded the same time, the record would not stand because Black riders were banned from the track.

November 26, 1896: On his eighteenth birthday, Marshall participates in his last amateur race, coming in fourteenth place.

December 5, 1896: The day before the big race in Madison Square Garden, Marshall participates in a series of sprints in the same venue. In his first pro race, the half-mile sprint, he beats crowd favorite and decorated sprint champion Eddie Bald. He wins the $100 prize and qualifies for the Six-Day Race.

December 7–12, 1896: The Six-Day Race takes place starting at midnight in Madison Square Garden. After the race, newspapers begin referring to Major as "The Black Cyclone," "The Worcester Whirlwind," and "The Ebony Flyer."

1898: Major holds seven records in various sprint categories.

August 10, 1899: Major wins the one-mile championship in Montreal, Canada, to become the first Black champion in cycling.

September 1900 (end of cycling season): Major sets world records in the half-mile and two-thirds-mile sprints. He becomes the American sprint champion at the end of the season, winning on points.

March–June 1901: Major finally competes in Europe. He was a religious man and did not compete on Sundays, which was when races were held in Europe. To accommodate the popular racer, the European circuit changed the race days so that Major could compete.

1901: Major wins forty-two of the fifty-seven races he enters.

1901: After losing the first match race (head-to-head race) against French champion Edmond Jacquelin, Major gets a quick rematch and wins.

1902: Major wins forty of the fifty-seven races he enters in Europe.

1902–04: Major races all over Europe, Australia, New Zealand, and the United States.

1905–06: Major takes a break from cycling due to physical and mental exhaustion.

1907: Major returns to racing.

1910: Marshall "Major" Taylor retires at the age of thirty-two.

BIBLIOGRAPHY

Balf, Todd. *Major: A Black Athlete, a White Era, and the Fight to Be the World's Fastest Human Being.* New York: Crown Publishing, 2009.

Cline-Ransome, Lesa. *Major Taylor: Champion Cyclist.* Illustrated by James Ransome. New York: Atheneum Books, 2004.

Kranish, Michael. *The World's Fastest Man: The Extraordinary Life of Cyclist Major Taylor, America's First Black Sports Hero.* New York: Scribner, 2019.

Major Taylor Association, Inc. https://majortaylorassociation.org.

Ritchie, Andrew. *Major Taylor: The Extraordinary Career of a Champion Bicycle Racer.* Baltimore: Johns Hopkins University Press, 1996.

Taylor, Marshall "Major." *The Fastest Bicycle Rider in the World.* Worcester, MA: Commonwealth Press, 1928.

Dedicated to my three champions:
Sabine, Adrian, and Sebastian
CRS

To Justin and Cory Williams, Katherine Towle Knox,
Rahsaan Bahati, Ayesha McGowan, Nelson Vails, and
to the memory of Sule Kangangi and Adé Hoghe
LE

First edition 2023

Library of Congress Catalog Card Number 2022922955
ISBN 978-1-5362-1498-7

23 24 25 26 27 28 APS 10 9 8 7 6 5 4 3 2 1

Printed in Humen, Dongguan, China

This book was typeset in Bauer Grotesk.
The illustrations were created digitally.

Candlewick Press
99 Dover Street
Somerville, Massachusetts 02144

www.candlewick.com